PRAISE FOR MIKE DOOLEY'S NOTES FROM THE UNIVERSE

"Your messages are uncanny; they all strike my heart, a chord of recognition and remembering of Truth, or expand into a little more of it. Thank you! It's amazing that such a widely distributed collection of words can effect an individual response in someone you haven't met! I suppose I'm sending you my appreciation for your service and contribution to 'consciousness,' specifically, supporting me in my journey of remembering and discovering."

"Your messages are so very uplifting. You will give much to a world that is hungry for this new light of truth."

"I just wanted to thank you for these messages. They are so insightful and really make me think—which is a very good thing. I always look forward to them. They definitely are playing a role in my spiritual growth. THANK YOU!"

"Thank you VERY much for the sentiment you sent today. By some miracle it was EXACTLY what I needed! I printed it out and posted it on my bulletin board to read hourly if need be!"

"Mike: Thank you again for making a difference in my life. You are a total inspiration that awakens my soul."

"Well, Mike, your e-mails bring me a solace of sorts . . . they are always good, and almost tear inducing. I truly cherish many of them. I even print them out and put them in my journal. I do appreciate such kind words. I am the sixteen-year-old who once wrote to you. Even at my age—with such ups and downs of emotion—your wisdom rings true and is truly a pickup for someone's feelings. Thank you again very much. Keep writing and observing and philosophizing. And I will, too."

"You had no way of knowing, of course, but your messages of encouragement and calls to action have helped to get me through a very difficult year. Thanks."

"Mike: I am truly enjoying these wonderful 'pearls'! All of your words echo my own feelings and knowledge. You are Heavenly!"

"Your messages continue to be an incredible inspiration. Thanks for being. I know that you have no way of knowing anything about the people who are on your e-mail list, but I will tell you that your last message hit me so on the money that I stopped and reread it three times. Mike, you should feel so very special that you have the ability to touch people this way. If each day you can 'shake or wake up' just one person, you accomplished a great thing. Thank you, thank you, thank you. Have a glorious day!"

"Mike, I just want to tell you, once again, how much I appreciate you, your insight, and your Mission. I know that the messages you send out take time and much effort on your part, and I want you to know that they help put the day into perspective. I have forwarded your messages many times, to friends all over the globe, and have received the same feedback from them that I am sending to you."

"Thank you, you are awesome. I am sure you know the profound effect you have on those of us lucky enough to receive your messages!"

"Dear Mike: I can't tell you how incredibly appropriate your messages are; they hit me at exactly the right time. It's very hard to believe that you don't write them especially for me. The synchronicity of the Universe never fails to impress me. Thank you. Blessed Be."

"Thanks so much for the continued positive comments and good wishes that you bring into my life . . . as well as to many, many others. I hope you realize how appreciated you are."

Notes

from the

Universe

NEW PERSPECTIVES
FROM AN OLD FRIEND

Mike Dooley

ATRIA BOOKS
New York London Toronto Sydney

BEYOND WORDS
PUBLISHING

ATRIA BOOKS
A Division of Simon & Schuster, Inc.
1230 Avenue of the Americas
New York, NY 10020

PUBLISHING
20827 N.W. Cornell Road, Suite 500
Hillsboro, Oregon 97124-9808
503-531-8700 / 503-531-8773 fax
www.beyondword.com

First Atria Books/Beyond Words hardcover edition September 2007

ATRIA BOOKS and colophon are trademarks of Simon & Schuster, Inc.

Beyond Words Publishing is a division of Simon & Schuster, Inc.

For more information about special discounts for bulk purchases,
please contact Simon & Schuster Special Sales at
1-800-456-6798 or business@simonandschuster.com.

Designed by Joel Avirom and Jason Snyder

Manufactured in the United States of America

1 3 5 7 9 10 8 6 4 2

Library of Congress Cataloging-in-Publication Data

Dooley, Mike.
Notes from the universe : new perspectives from an old friend / Mike Dooley.
p. cm.
1. Self-help techniques—Miscellanea. 2. Spirituality—Miscellanea.
3. Occultism—Miscellanea. I. Title.
BF1999.D6155 2007
158—dc22   2007017573

ISBN-13: 978-1-58270-176-9
ISBN-10:   1-58270-176-8

The corporate mission of Beyond Words Publishing, Inc.: *Inspire to Integrity*

For Amanda

INTRODUCTION

I used to think everyone knew something that I didn't. They, like me, weren't aware of what it was, and they didn't seem to notice that I was without it, but to me the difference was painful. I felt awkwardly different, which led to a burning desire to question the things that most people seem to take for granted. A desire to know what life is about, which I have now largely satisfied, making the price of my sensed alienation very small in comparison.

I didn't realize it at the time, but my desire to "know" had put me on a path of *inner* knowing; or better, my thinking was beginning to attract like thinking. It seemed my questions were slowly answering themselves, opening my eyes to the insights I now realize are latent within us all. I was never sure just when my "illuminations" took place until sometime after the fact, as if an intuitive knowing had been imparted when I wasn't paying close attention.

By the time I was twenty, I had deduced that we're not just here accidentally, nor were we set adrift by some angry god who would then judge, condemn, and sentence us before we even understood what was going on. I believed that through *thinking*, we are *creators*, the joyful gladiators of the Universe revered for daring the ultimate dare; here of our own choosing, each of us for our own extraordinarily unique reasons, foremost among which is for the sheer adventure of doing so. And if there was ever proof that I was on the right track, the fact that I now spend part of every day writing for "the Universe" is it.

In 1989, these were the kinds of thoughts Mom, my brother, and I put on our company's brand-new line of T-shirts, TUT® (Totally Unique Thoughts®), our philosophy being that everyone is special, that every life is meaningful, and that we're all here to learn that dreams really do come true. We did real well, eventually selling over one million of them.

But as the year 2000 dawned, with both our sales and our enthusiasm waning, we decided to close the last of our stores and liquidate our remaining inventory. Reluctantly, I briefly hit the pavement with my accountant's résumé in hand. Fortunately, no one was hiring (at least not me!), and fortunately again, I had enough money from our T-shirt days to coast for several years. Even more fortunately, I still had a thousand or so people looking forward to receiving my free "Monday Morning Motivators" via e-mail each week.

So I decided that as long as I didn't have to "work" yet, I'd keep doing the one thing that filled me with the greatest sense of accomplishment and purpose—write, about the truths *I* most needed to embrace to change *my* life. And figure out how to make it pay, later.

Talk about scary. As the months rolled by, there were plenty of nights I tossed, literally in a sweat, thinking "*What* am I doing with my life? What went wrong? How am I going to make any money at this? What if I have to sell my home? What if I can't find a job and no one will buy my home? What if? What if? What if . . . ?" And day after day, week after week, month after month, my reserves dwindled, and *nothing* came in.

But I knew a trick. I knew that figuring out "the hows" wasn't really my job; they belonged to the

Universe. I also knew to focus on the end result, the kind of life I wanted, and to get busy turning over every stone, knocking on every door, following every impulse, so that theoretically, at least, the Universe could take care of the details.

Whaaaaa! Has it ever!!! Somehow, during all the knocking and turning and visualizing, I acted on enough hunches and instincts to keep me buoyed with the necessary optimism to press on and not look back. And literally, the next thing I knew, TUT's Adventurers Club was born and the Universe began using e-mail. At last count, solely from word-of-mouth advertising, 150,000 people in 174 countries now receive *Notes from the Universe* five days a week. At times, I can hardly believe the swift reversal and rise of my good fortune. I now have two wildly popular audio programs, a three-book deal with a major publisher, private speaking invitations, "boatloads" of people who join me on cruises, an appearance in *The Secret*, world tours, and a subscriber base that's still growing exponentially.

Even for me, it's almost hard to believe that this turn of events wasn't somehow meant to be, but I know better. I remember all too well the forks

that lay in the road just seven years ago and how
"career" certainty and monetary gains were virtually
nonexistent, tempting me to run for safety down
paths that promised little else. But as I now tell my
audiences: If you understand the nature of reality,
that our thoughts unfailingly become the things and
events of our lives, if you let go of the past and *move*
with your dreams, it will *always* be *enough*.

The Notes in this book are designed to shed
light on your own *inner* path: to spark your memory,
attract like thinking, and awaken the slumbering
deity within. They contain the truths I've come
to know and live by about who we are, why we're
here, and the magic at our disposal. Everything I've
discovered is neatly tucked between the paragraphs,
and for the eager, earnest reader, far more meaning
will be found therein than will first meet the eye.

To the life of *your* dreams,

HOW YOU MIGHT
USE THIS BOOK

When these Notes were first sent out by e-mail to subscribers, the most common reply I received (and still receive, endlessly) was that more often than not, day after day, readers were amazed by the uncanny timing of each Note as it related to exactly where they were in their respective lives. "How could you know? Even my closest friends don't have a clue!" or "I was eating French toast at 4 a.m. when today's Note arrived . . . and I *had* to call and wake my mother to share that the PS asked, 'More syrup?' just as I was reaching for it!" or "As I was worrying about the sad ending of my marriage and its potential effect on my children, tears and tissues everywhere, today's Note arrived telling me 'If you only knew just how incredibly well everything is going to turn out, for you and those close to you, right now you'd likely feel light as a feather, free as the wind, happy, confident, giddy . . .'"

How, indeed? The obvious answer is that while 150,000 people receive the exact same Note, they each interpret it 150,000 different ways, filtered through their own thoughts and circumstances. The not-so-obvious answer is that in the jungles of time and space, things are *not* as they appear. We've been told since our lives began that we are but mere bystanders to the glory of life and that everything happens along a rigid, linear timeline. The truth, however, is that we're each the co-creator of all that we share, and our experiences spring from an eternal now. It's only our exclusive reliance upon our physical senses to interpret life that makes this so challenging to grasp. And so, just as those who witness a beautiful sunrise actually *participate* in its co-creation, so too in some mystical, magical way are the readers of these words and the daily Notes their co-creators—whether they were received as an e-mail in the "past" or randomly chosen from the pages now before you.

Go on, give it a try. Just open this book to any "random" page and see what you get. You're really quite the writer, you know.

*If I told you there have been
no mistakes,*
that I understand every decision you've ever made,
and that the challenges you've faced, you've faced
for everyone, would you listen?

If I told you that what you dream of, I dream of for you,
that the only things "meant to be" are what you decide
upon, and that all that stands between you and the life
of your dreams are the thoughts you choose
to think, would you try to understand?

And if I told you that you are never alone,
that there are angels who sing your name in praise,
and that I couldn't possibly be any more proud of you
than I already am, would you believe me?

Would you? Even if I pulled your leg, made you blush,
and winked between the lines?

Then I shall . . .

Notes
from the
Universe

It's me, the Universe.

I've got good news and bad news.

The good news is that you've passed the audition!

Yee-haa! You've earned your wings! You're a certified, bona fide Being of Light, capable of transcending all fears and manifesting all dreams. From here on out, you have but to dwell upon what you want, and I must bring it forth.

The bad news is that this message was supposed to have reached you eons and eons ago.

Sorry.

Do you have any idea . . .
of how powerful you REALLY are?

Do you have any idea
of how far your thoughts reach?

Do you have any idea
of how many lives you've already touched?

Do you have any idea
of how much you've already accomplished?

Do you?

Ever wonder
how many angels you have?

All of them.

They insisted.

Whether it's praise, love, criticism, money, time, space, power, punishment, sorrow, laughter, care, pain, or pleasure . . . the more you give, the more you will receive.

Today, you are a magnet . . .
for infinite abundance, divine intelligence, and
unlimited love.

Actually, this has always been true.

Anyone watching you?

Good. This is a double-secret exercise.

Pretend you just received a phone call with wonderful, mind-blowing, life-changing news!

As you put down the receiver, your arms fly up over your head with joy. Pumping fists, then waving palms, like you just crossed a finish line before throngs of adoring fans. You cover your face with your hands, trying to contain the euphoria, but it doesn't work, so you reach for the sky again while shaking your head in disbelief. You're grinning, crying, and just so happy!

Yes! Life is awesome, and you feel so grateful!!!!!!!

Got it?

Now if someone catches you doing this, just tell 'em it was your pet psychic who called, and they'll forget everything they just saw.

The Universe xxoo

PS—Show me what you want to feel, create the feeling within yourself, and I'll then orchestrate the circumstances, however outlandish, that will help you feel it again, and again, and again.

Turn the jungles
of time and space . . . into a patio garden . . .
by realizing that their many mysteries actually
conspire on your behalf.

To better understand
who you really are, understand why you want
what you want, getting to the emotions you seek.

To go even deeper . . . ask yourself why you think
you can't feel those now.

Life is like a dance

and we're partners. Setbacks, delays, and detours?
Heck, they're just like some of the steps in the
mambo, tango, and cha-cha. If you dissected the
movements and saw them without regard to the rest
of the dance, everyone would look like total dorks.
But when you see the big picture . . .
poetry in motion.

In life, setbacks, delays, and detours are often just
my way of "keeping" you for something way better.
Don't let them discourage you, don't lose faith,
and whatever you do, don't stop dancing.

Your most able choreographer,

The Universe

PS—You choose the dance, the ballroom,
or the disco, and let me write the steps, 'kay?

It's *not* hard.

Time and space are the playground of the Universe, not the Harvard of the Universe.

Kindergarten dressed as paradise, at recess.

Bogged down,

spinnin' your wheels, out of time, frustrated, stressin'? It's the details. You're messin' with the details, which is a million times worse than messin' with Texas.

Messin' with the details is like trying to play tennis with a golf club, like trying to cook with yesterday's hot stove, or trying to find meaningful new friends at the mall wearing a chicken suit.

Just get clear on your vision—the end result. Think, think, and let go. Follow your impulses, do what you can, act as if, and know you've done your part.

The Universe is the detail Queen, a perfectionist extraordinaire. Delegate.

Brock? (chickenspeak)

PS—Of course, there is a time and a place for chicken suits, just not in Texas.

PPS—Remember what was just said about the details.

One of your greatest challenges
is realizing that the hurdles of time and space
are simply reflections of imagined hurdles.

See no problems.

Was it you?!

We have some new "help" here, and our incoming correspondence has been kind of garbled.

Someone was thinking big, I mean really big, and now the entire Universe has been thrown into action, aligning players, circumstances, and coincidences that will miraculously fall into just the right place at just the right time. It's changed everything, absolutely everything. The world will never be the same.

Actually, this happens with your every thought. But if it was you, did you mean joy when you said toy?

Sounded like you wanted every toy? Either way, consider it done, just let us know.

Tallyho,*

The Universe

PS—What are you gonna do with a piece of earth?

*Tallyho! (British for "After the fox!"; Adventurese for "Until we meet again . . .")

13

You *do* have time.

Someone bugging you?

Nah, way too easy.

Just like happiness,
disappointment is an "inside" job.

Can you keep a secret?

You know the space between you and all things, the void. Like right now, the space between you and this book.

That's where I hide . . . and watch.

Looking to see what your expectations are: of yourself, others, abundance, health, and happiness. And from this space . . . as I catch your thoughts, hear your words, and see all you do, no matter where we are . . . I manifest the next moment in time.

Tallyho,

The Universe

PS—If you reach out now, into this space, you can feel me. I'm here. It's true. You're never alone.

All that you *must* do,
you've already done.

Pssst . . . It's me again . . .
the Universe.

You deserve more, you know, much more.

And I just happen to have "some." Imagine.

Try this. STOP trying to predict, and therefore limit, where it's going to come from. Just know it's going to come and let me figure out the rest.

Cool?

By the way, you rock.

Shhhhh . . .

Do you realize
that the Universe cannot have, do, and be
more . . . unless you have, do, and be more?

Want it all.

(As if you didn't.)

It's easy to look around
at all the people who already have what you want,
notice how they differ from you, and then think that
they are the "kind of people" for whom having what
you want comes naturally. Whereas you are not,
otherwise you'd have it too.

Very rational thinking, and a super way for
nonadventurers to avoid responsibility, rest on the
sidelines, and watch more TV.

Adventurers, on the other hand, understand that
they are exactly the kind of people who should have
the things they want. Otherwise, they wouldn't be
blessed with wanting them.

Sure, there may be a lot
of "real estate" between here and where
you dream of being, but the road, if you
notice, happens to run straight through
the middle of paradise.

Wouldn't you just know it?!

You go to earth for a little adventure, some fun and games, some learning and growing, and the next thing you know, you're trapped in a sea of illusions, trying to figure everything out with a little human brain, sweating the details, and desperately seeking approval and appreciation.

Sounds like reality TV.

Here's what you do . . . No, you don't vote everyone off. You just remember how things really work.

You remember that the thoughts you choose to focus on, from this day forward, will become the things and events of the rest of your life, no matter where you've been, no matter what anyone else says, and no matter how scary things may seem to be.

Behold, a new day . . .
with rainbows, sunshine, and blue skies.
New players, rebounds, and recoveries.
Abundance, health, and harmony . . . just like
you've been picturing them, right?

Right?!

Please tell me you've been picturing them!!

You are "here" (your life now)
and you want to go "there" (your dreamed-of life).
And because both are physical places, it would seem
that you must manipulate the physical world to
go from "here" to "there."

Aha! This is the ultimate illusion.

Physical places are simply mirages, reflections,
of an inner world, the world of your thoughts.
So to get from "here" to "there" you must do
your manipulating within.

A thought worth dwelling on—brought to you
by your friend, the Universe.

To find the shortest path
to any dream, work with ideas, not facts. Dwell
upon the end result, not the hows. And rely upon
the Universe, not yourself.

Hidden excerpt

from *Illumination for Dummies: Time~Space Edition.*
Now a best seller in dimensions far, far away . . .

It's like, between every single second of the day,
there's a pause. Life is suspended. Frozen and
unfrozen. Imperceptible to the physical senses because
these moments and non-moments are all strung
together by your thoughts, beliefs, and intents, which
span the gaps, creating a complete and seamless
picture. It's even happening now, between every
word you've just read.

It's during these pauses that the future is forged.
And just as all things flicker like a firefly, so does time,
during which the Universe is busy at work, flying into
action, moving mountains, plotting circumstances, and
planning coincidences, unrestrained by the limits
of material existence, including cause and effect.
This is where the magic lies.

Each succeeding physical moment then reflects
the creations of the previous non-physical
moment, dependent not upon what has existed
in the physical, but upon the usually slow evolution
of your beliefs, intents, and expectations that
carry through both realities.

(Are you sitting down?)

The past can even be rewritten and memories inserted, so that never a beat is missed. (Scratch "can even be," and use "are often." Just pacing you to ward off brain freeze.)

Next time you want something, play off these pauses, not time and space. Don't look to the physical, look to the unseen. And dwell in the realm of infinite possibilities.

But you knew that.

Tallyho, ho, ho,

The Universe

PS—It goes on to say that the evolution spoken of need not be slow.

There is no greater weapon . . .
than kindness.

A smile, a compliment, encouragement, and compassion belong in the arsenal of every Time~Space Adventurer.

Today, may you crush, kill, and destroy the fears you encounter, in others and in yourself.

En garde.

The root of every "evil"
is looking to time and space for meaning,
for solutions, for identity; for friends, love,
and laughter; wealth, health, and harmony.

The source of all things—material things—is spirit,
which is molded by thought (yours) and then,
without judgment, impressed upon matter before
your very eyes. Trying to get what you want, no
matter what it is, by looking to time and space first
is like putting the cart before the horse and will
leave you feeling powerless, heartbroken, even sick.

And dear heart, this is the candy-coated
version of the truth.

Tallyho,

The Universe

Isn't it strange,
how once you set your "gaze" upon something
or someone, you get to decide what you'll see:
good, bad, or ugly. Yet still, you think "it," or "they,"
has something to do with your feelings and moods?

Don't fight it.

Behold, a Being of Light,
radiant, illuminated, and full of grace. Come
to lift humanity higher into the light. All bow
and sing praise . . . Agh! It's you! What are you
doing back in time and space?

Aha. I see. Pretending. Well, that's perfectly
understandable. We all need to pretend
once in a while.

So how's it going?

Yes, indeed, challenges. Part and parcel of any
worthwhile adventure.

Tell me—there's a rumor that in time and space,
the illusions are soooooo captivating, the coffee
soooooo rich, and the chocolate soooooo dark,
it's easy to forget you're just making it all up and
that all you have to do to awaken is to pretend your
way to wherever it is you'd like to go?

Cream and sugar?

Always . . .
that which you most need is already at hand.

It's simply your incessant searching and belief
in its absence that keeps it from view.

When you get there,
wherever "there" is for you, probably nothing else
will matter more than wanting to help others
achieve as you have.

Who will you first reach out to? What will you do
or say? How will you conduct yourself in public?
How will you show them what you see?

Better start practicing.

The only difference
between a friend and a foe is that you've decided
where love can grow.

There isn't a soul on the planet who doesn't crave
your approval.

A question
from your friend the Universe:

Just how much time do you spend thinking big?
I mean really, *really* BIG?

Good, very good! Because that's exactly
how much of "it" you're going to get!

What a coincidence.

Your "challenges"
are simply the manifestation of your so-called
invisible, limiting beliefs.

Not so invisible after all, eh?

Do you realize,
that you have never heard anything,
from anyone, that you did not want to hear?

Pretty tricky of you.

Dearest Dear Heart,

I'm sorry to write you like this, but it's just
not enough that you tell me you adore me.
That you love my mysterious ways and that
you're brimming with excitement for the
infinite possibilities that lay before us.
It's simply not enough, not for me and not
for you. Pumpkin, you must show me.

You must go out into the world and greet
each day with faith that I am with you.
Engage the magic.

Stride confidently into your affairs
expecting a miracle, and go boldly in the
direction of your dreams.

Darling, it's time to ratchet things up a notch.
Time to play, too, to take everything less
seriously, to get our "groove on," because
there's simply nothing, nothing, nothing that
we cannot do together . . . though it's you,
Sunshine, who must set us in motion.

Yours till the end of time,

The Universe

PS—You know, just do that thing you do,
the one that drives me wild. Be all of you . . .
and the rest will happen naturally.

Uga-chug-a, uga-chug-a, uga-chug-a.

Just yesterday,

I was taking some time off, soaring through
the sky, spread-eagle style, flying between some
mammoth cumulus clouds, when—BAM—
I flew into a stork on a delivery run. Always loved
storks, so simple, so accepting.

Felt bad for the poor fellow, so we flew together
awhile and I chatted him up. I didn't tell him

I was the Universe.

You know what he told me?

He said there are no accidents.

"None?" I asked, feigning surprise.

"None."

"Well, then, it sure was a nice coincidence running
into you like this." And after sputtering a bit,
he said there were none of those either.

"None?"

"Nope."

I asked him how he knew so much about life, being a stork and all. And he said there was a little bit of the divine in all of us; that we all know the truth about reality, and that by focusing on any problem or question, the answer is drawn to you.

"Get out of here," I told him.

"No, really. Take today. I was wondering where all these babies came from, when—BAM—suddenly, from nowhere, I just knew."

Never trust appearances.

Do you want to know
what the world starts looking like when
you start moving with an understanding
that you are a sublime Being of Light?

When you start realizing that you are
the master of your destiny?

Knowing that all things are possible and
that the Universe does conspire tirelessly
on your behalf?

Yeah, pretty much the way it looks right now.

You simply have to change
your worldview—your opinions and beliefs—
in order to change your experience.

Tricky? Maybe.

Worth the effort? Depends.

How badly do you want greater peace of mind,
more friends and laughter, health, and comfort,
and enough abundance to never have to ask,
"How much?"

It's not real! Don't go there!

The things and events of time and space are
like Play-doh; fictional, make-believe.

What matter are what you feel in your heart
and the dreams that flit through your head.
This is the ultimate test, to discover what's real
in a sea of illusions.

You can do it or you wouldn't be here.
Don't look to the world for clues, not even
to your family, friends, or career. Look within.
You decide what's right. You decide what's possible.
You write the script and lay down the laws.
You are the door, the path, and the light.

The things and events
of time and space . . . the stuff that's
surrounding you now, your memory of recent
events, all simply reveal where you've been,
not where you're headed.

If there was just one thing
I could tell you about living the life of your
dreams, knowing that if you understood it,
it would be "enough," I would ask you to realize
that you already are.

Would a loving parent
ever give a child a story to read that didn't have a
wonderfully happy ending?

No. Never. But they might add, "Whatever you do,
don't stop reading at the scary parts!"

Your invisible limiting beliefs
are only invisible when you live within
their limits—or when you keep on doing what
you've always been doing.

Push yourself. Dare yourself to think bigger,
to reach, and to behave as if a dream or two of
yours has already manifested. Then you'll see 'dem
little buggers pop out of the woodwork, painted
fluorescent orange, loaded to the teeth with logic,
imploring you to turn around and go back to safety!

Do something, do it today, something you
wouldn't normally do. Like maybe . . . take off
early from work and go to a matinee movie.

Aha! Did you just see a couple of 'em?!

Be warned: Sometimes, once exposed, they'll try
to snuggle up to you, looking sooo innocent
and adorable. And as if that wasn't bad enough,
they'll start with their "baby talk." Sickening.

Impatience is what you feel
when you think the future—in hours, days,
or years—will be "better" than the present.

It won't.

If you only knew,
just how incredibly well everything is going to
turn out, for you and those close to you, right now
you'd likely feel light as a feather, free as the wind,
happy, confident, giddy.

Whoops, kind of let the cat out of the bag there.

Well, now you know.

Invariably

when big dreams come true, and I mean BIG,
there is a total metamorphosis of one's life.
Thoughts change. Words change. Decisions
are made differently. Gratitude is tossed about
like rice at a wedding. Priorities are rearranged,
and optimism soars. Yeah, those folks
are almost annoying.

You could have guessed all that, huh?

Would you have guessed that these changes,
invariably, come about before, not after,
the dream's manifestation?

Invariably means always.

Know what's missing
from most people's lives?

The realization that nothing is
missing from their lives.

When you look into the mirror each morning, do you apply your makeup or shaving cream to your reflection in the glass?

Ha! Of course not; you'd be locked up. Instead, you go to the source of the reflection.

So then, when it comes to living the life of your dreams, the same philosophy should apply. Why try to manipulate the illusions of time and space when you can go to their source, the inner world of your own thoughts, beliefs, and expectations, where the real work is done anyway?

Challenges in life

don't arise haphazardly, no matter how accidental or coincidental they may seem. They only arrive when you're ready for them.

Not when you're ready to be squashed, but when you're ready to grow, overcome, and be more than who you were before they arrived.

The reason that some
of your thoughts haven't yet become things . . .
is because other thoughts of yours have.

Adventurer Alert

Remember . . . You are an intergalactic, indestructible, unstoppable eternal Being of Light, and for the time being, you're just pretending to be the little "hottie" holding this book.

Okay?

The Universe

Ahhhhh, let's see here, whose day shall I make? Whose week? Year? Entire life? Whose thoughts shall I endow with the power to become all things? Who will be made invincible to every challenge, and who shall I catapult over every obstacle? Who will get a second chance, a third chance? No, not enough. Whose "life reset button" shall I hit whenever they want a "do-over"? Who will eat their cake, and have it too????

Oh, there I go again. Fantasizing, pretending, wishing it was really me who gets to decide such things—dang it. Wishing I could bestow such blessings, instead of just being the "techie" behind the scenes allowed to perform my miracles and magic only when called upon and believed in. It's like I'm life's Maytag repairman.

Use me. Please. So that I may fill your every cup, grant your every wish, and harvest your every dream. And let's begin today.

Guess I had to let that out.

Love you, whatever you choose,

The Universe

PS—It couldn't possibly be any easier than it is.

The best way to deal
with other people . . . is to just
let them be other people.

After all, that's how you want
them to deal with you.

Shhhhh . . .

The secret to living the life of your dreams
is to start living the life of your dreams, at once,
to any degree that you possibly can.

Just do it.

Everything you need to know, you know, and everything you need to have, you have. Everything!

Time and Space is a primitive school. There are bigger challenges "out there," bigger adventures, and lots more friends, but you gotta do what you gotta do, here and now. You gotta live the truths you've discovered, apply the principles, and never again think, "Why isn't it working?" "It's hard," "I don't know," because such thoughts are like hitting the replay button for whatever you've just been through. Look ahead with your dreams in mind and give thanks, because you know exactly what to do.

Phew . . . feel better?

Tallyho, ho, ho!

As powerful as you are . . .
whose day are you going to make today?

What if you did have the power, the reach, and the glory? What if you were given dominion over all things? And what if eternity lay before you, brimming with love, friends, and laughter?

Yet still, one day, in all your radiance, bubbling over with giddy excitement, you tripped, fell, and got hurt. Really badly hurt.

Would you hate yourself? Would you give up on your dreams? Would you forget about your power, your reach, and the glory?

Oh, come now . . .

Thinking . . .
is the ultimate contact sport.

All things considered . . .
you've never really asked for much.

Hey, what's up with that?

Everything matters.

Worldwide Proclamation!

This is to remind all my loyal subjects that you are not my loyal subjects. And that I'm bloody tired of all the sacrifices, appeasements, and groveling.

I, the Universe—the sun, the moon, and the stars, the Alpha and the Omega, and all the rest—have created a paradise in Time and Space so that I, through you, might experience its infinite splendors, drink from its every cup, and live, love, and be merry in ways impossible without you.

Your desires are my desires for you. What you want and when you want it, these were my ideas, too. Your dreams are my dreams. You are the be-all and end-all of Time and Space, the only reason for this Garden of Eden. You can do no wrong, there are no mistakes, and it's all good.

Follow your heart, delight in your preferences. Approve of yourself. Stake your claim, demand it, and hold out your hands. Banish your doubts, get off of your knees, and live as you please. Because, dearest, you can, and this is all I ever wanted.

With unspeakable love, I am,

The Universe

PS—ROAAAAAAAAAAAAAR!

Jambo*! Universe here . . .

Golly, do I ever need a vacation.

Can you imagine having the entire world spin in the palm of your hand? Writing the script to history? Being able to change the course of eternity by just changing your mind? Kind of far-out, isn't it? But it's all right here in the brochure. Read it myself, "Spellbinding! Intoxicating! The ultimate escape! Join billions on an unforgettable adventure into the jungles of Time and Space, to a paradise found where you are master of your destiny, all things are possible, and your every thought changes everything. So real, you may even forget who you are!"

Perfect for me, bags are packed.

Be cool (just brushing up on the lingo),

The Universe

PS—Let's do lunch.

*Jambo! (Swahili for "hello"; Adventurese for "I'm glad our paths have crossed . . .")

It's not so much

about having faith in yourself. Way too hard.
Besides, you can wrestle that croc after you
move mountains.

For now, just have faith in me, in the magic,
and in the unseen, and it shall be done.

Tallyho,

The Universe

Never underestimate
the Universe.

Here's a little trick
on how to change the scenery in your life radically,
fantastically, and, perhaps, forever.

(If that's what you really want.)

Look the other way.

Adventurers Global Advisory

"Staying the course" should not be confused with clinging to a cursed "how."

Oh, "it's" not working?

Well, do you know where you'd be right now, what your life would be like, if it wasn't working?

Not reading this, for one. About half as good-looking as you now are, two. And perhaps wondering, in a strictly spiritual sense, who let the dogs out.

The Universe

PS—It is working. And it's getting easier. And you *are* getting better, and better, and better.

Whatever you'd like to know,
you already know.

Be still.

If you knew for certain

that very, very soon all your dreams would be coming true, what would you do today to prepare the way? (Do it.)

How might you celebrate? (Do this, too.)

Who would you tell? (Write them a brief note, now; you don't have to mail it yet.)

What thoughts of gratitude would you have? (Express them.)

And finally, who would you help to "achieve," as you have achieved? (Help them.)

Whosoever may torment you,
harass you, confound you, or upset you is a teacher.

Not because they're wise, but because you
seek to become so.

It all goes by so fast,
doesn't it?

One minute you're here, and the next you're gone.

So really, you've got nothing to lose, have you?
Nothing! You're gonna make it "home" anyway.
You're gonna be exalted, and it's gonna be
so glorious, happy, and easy.

Then, after a careful life review, you're gonna slap
your hand on your celestial forehead, jump up and
down with uproarious laughter, and say, "Dang,
my thoughts really did become the things and events
of my life. That little book was right. And as exalted
as I am here, I was there. And as easy as it is here,
so could it have been there! I wanna play again,
I wanna go back. This time I promise not to forget.
I promise I'll believe in my dreams and myself.
I'll never let go. I'll never give up. I'll keep the faith.
Really I will."

Actually, it's pretty simple.

You have one real choice: To do your best,
with what you have, from where you are.

Everything else is just stalling.

It's not possible!

You cannot significantly change your life, for better or for worse, by manipulating the material world. Not by working harder, not by studying longer, not by schmoozing, not by sweating, not by fasting, not by the hair of your chinny chin chin.

But change, great change, is inescapable when you first begin manipulating the world of your thoughts, which weigh a whole lot less than material things anyway.

It's that simple.

You are the reason
the sun came up today.

Believe it.

Don't wait for those feelings
of excitement, confidence, and expectation that
will come when your life suddenly takes off,
because your life cannot suddenly take off until
you first have those feelings of excitement,
confidence, and expectation.

(Heck, if you have to, just pretend. Make
believe, fake it. Right now, get up, walk down
the hall, smile, wave, wink, pump your fist,
and exude all over the place!)

Some Investment Advice
from the Universe

Did you follow your hunches during the '90s in the stock market? Did you hear what I was telling you about huge yields in real estate? Did you "stumble" across those itty-bitty public companies with stock offerings that made penny investors millionaires?

Phew, I was slammed doling out golden opportunities to anyone I could reach. It became kind of a hobby, you know, to fill in the gaps of boredom that go along with being the Universe.

Truthfully, though, you didn't miss a thing. Those fortunes were chicken feed compared to what I offer on a full-time basis through my day job. Are you ready for real opportunity? Do you even have room for the returns? No, you don't. But that's a good problem.

Thought. That's right. Thought is the greatest vehicle of all time for burying one's self, family, and friends in wealth and abundance—no matter what's going on with the economy.

Thoughts have their own economy, and now is
a super-great time to get in on the ground floor.
With my patented trade secrets, I can take any old
invisible thought of yours and turn it into a mine
of gold, a mountain of cash, a well of prosperity.

It's not too late! The best is yet to come.
Invest in thought, follow your hunches, and live
the life of your dreams.

Public disclosure: This offer is irrevocable.
You're now an investor whether you know it or not.
All of your thoughts will become things. No lawyers
can help you. Save yourself; choose the good ones.

No matter how great
the temptation . . . (I'm talking about the
temptation you're feeling right this very second),
no matter how great . . .

STOP seeing yourself as just human!

You are pure energy, with an infinite reach.

Wait a minute!

What does being a better you have to do with anything?

Nothing! You're already smarter, kinder, more honest, insightful, and ambitious, even better looking, than 99.99 percent of the people who now live in abundance, health, and harmony. True? You know it is!

It's not about being a better you, nor even a more deserving you. It's about knowing you're already both.

What will it take for you

to begin having full-time faith that there does indeed
exist a magical Universe that is, at this very moment,
conspiring on your behalf?

How about your ability to read my thoughts,
right now, by deciphering these little blue
squiggles on the page?

How about the fact that right now, billions
of atoms and cells are busy whirling about,
while holding you together?

How about the fact that your heart has beat
some twenty-two times, without your help,
since you began reading this page?

How about all the lucky coincidences and
happy accidents that have brought you friends
who now love you and adventures to thrill,
with more of both on the horizon?

How about the fact that the sun rose
this morning so that you might have
another day in paradise?

Hul-lo?

There's nothing you can ask for
that won't set the entire Universe in motion.

Nothing. Nothing. Nothing.

Courageous is the soul
who ventures into time and space to learn
of their divinity. For while they cannot lose,
they can think they have, and the loss will seem
intolerable. And while they cannot fail, they can
think they have, and the pain will seem unbearable.
And while they cannot ever be less than they
truly are—powerful, eternal, and loved—they can
think they are, and all hope will seem lost.

And therein lies their test. A test of perceptions:
of what to focus on, of what to believe in,
in spite of appearances.

Courageous indeed . . . the pride of the Universe,
and I should know.

Never compromise a dream.

Do what you must. The fears, beasts,
and mountains before you are part of
the plan; stepping-stones to a promised land;
to a time and place that is so much closer
than you even suspect.

Don't let your eyes deceive, for even as you
read these words, your ship swiftly approaches.

Can you imagine
actually being embarrassed by the enormity
of wealth and abundance you've acquired?
By the peace and harmony that pervade your life?
By the ease and simplicity of everything you do?
Almost feeling the need to apologize to those
in your life who have yet to awaken and harness
the principles that are free to all?

Start.

What if, this very moment,
you realized you were dreaming? Dreaming you
were at home, at work, wherever you now are,
and that you were reading this Note. And in that
dream you also realized that as real as it all seemed,
there was also a greater reality from which you were
dreaming and a greater essence that is yourself. That
you came from eternity and will return to eternity,
and that, in truth, you are your dream weaver.

Then suddenly it dawned on you that you could
not awaken from this dream until you first
demonstrated this revelation by claiming
responsibility for your every manifestation
heretofore and exercising dominion over all things.

Yeeeehaaaaaaaaaaaaaaaaaaa!

Just like before . . .

it's gonna happen when you least expect it,
from where you least expect it,
and how you least expect it.

So forget about it. Except, of course,
to remember that it's gonna happen.

Have you ever wondered . . .
at how you might change, once some of your
grandest dreams are realized?

About how you'd behave differently if you
already had a fabulous house on the lake,
or if you were suddenly surrounded by mobs
of loving and adoring friends?

You'd saunter. Yep, when you walked outside your
home, through the 'hood, grocery store, or office,
you'd saunter. You'd even saunter inside your home.

So start sauntering. Get into it.
And maybe start winking, too.

Not only will people notice your calm,
your grace, and your confidence, but so will I.

Of all the people,
in all the world, not a single one of them . . .
is more precious, loved, and deserving than you.

You are creation's
first and last chance . . . to be you. Just as you are
today. That's all you have to be.

Bask. It's more than enough.

It's always best
to assume that everyone either knows
the truth or will know the truth, because
either they do or they will.

What if there really was
a Santa Claus, an Easter Bunny, or a God who picked
and chose among those whose prayers He answered,
who got to decide who was ready for what and who
judged those He would either save or damn?

I know, I know!

Everyone could spend the rest of their lives
hoping, wishing, and asking, instead of doing,
being, and having.

Tallyho, ho, ho!

PS—Think we'll get any presents
this year after that one?

Yo! This is the Universe,
and have I got great news!

I've just finished distributing the Powerball earnings and have lots and lots of time and energy and abundance left over. (You wouldn't even believe how much if I told you.) Here's what I'm thinking:

How would you like more money, more time, and more friends? Yes?! Well, that's exactly what I've been working on!

Now, here's what you can do. At some point today, or during the week, take out a pen and paper (or use your computer if you like) and write a letter to someone who lives far away. Someone you love and respect, and share the "news" with them. I want you to write this letter as if these dreams of yours have already transpired, and I want you to tell them the whole enchilada. Write down every detail. Share with them your astonishment, the ramifications, and describe your happiness so that they (and I) can feel your emotions. Then save that letter for when you really need it.

Hokey? Absolutely! A powerful act of thought and faith that will affect the course of your life. Yes! Yes! Yes! Yes! Yes! Yes! Yes!

The longer the letter, and the greater the details, the more powerful the effect.

Your humble servant,

The Universe

For all the reasons
that you might draw someone into your life . . .
one would never be to find their faults.

Always, do what you can.

Because once you at least do what you can, no matter how seemingly insignificant, everything changes.

Don't just see the magic,
engage it! Challenge it! Dare it! Dream big, with
every expectation that your dreams will manifest.

Demand that they come true! You're not beholden
to life. Life is beholden to you. You are its reason for
being. You came first.

Do you realize that everyone,
absolutely everyone on this planet—grumpy office
workers, arguing children, fickle spouses, the
"narrow-minded," the extremists—all think
they're doing their very best?

So how do you get through to someone who
thinks they're doing their very best?

How would someone get through to you?

Have you been there?

To that place of quiet bliss, of knowing that you're doing enough, wishing for nothing except what already is, exactly as it is, seeing the blue in the sky like you've never seen it before, watching a butterfly as if it appeared just for you, feeling so light that you're sure you could float, understanding the trials and tribulations of days gone by and being glad for every single one of them, feeling so wrapped up in the present that you couldn't care less about tomorrow, knowing that you're provided for, that the manifestation of your dreams is inevitable, and that the Universe flat-out adores you, reveres you, and wants for nothing, except to see your smile and hear your laughter?

That's right, very good, dearest. You're there now.

Adventurers All-Points Bulletin

We interrupt your day to remind you that time is fleeting. Seconds, minutes, and hours are completely vanishing. Right now, here today, you are the spring chick of your tomorrows.

Cluck, baby.

Thank you.

I need your help with this one.

Please, just for a second, hold out the palm of your hand and give it a quick glance. Now imagine a miniaturized version of a loved one carefully and comfortably resting in it. Feel waves of your love blanketing this precious being. Imagine seeing the life of this loved one playing out in your palm and feeling their every joy and sadness. Imagine reading his or her mind and wanting nothing for yourself except to see their dreams come true.

Then you smile radiantly, filled with pride and joy, knowing that they are always safe, always provided for, never alone, and inescapably destined to learn of these truths for themselves. You smile because you know that the day of their awakening swiftly approaches, as does their own sublime joy and the manifestation of their boldest dreams.

Okay, that should do it.

Now, can you also imagine that "someone else" right this very moment is smiling down at you as you play out your life in the palm of their hand?

Yours truly,

The Universe

If it's hard,
there's something you're missing.

Let's play doctor:
I'll be the doctor.

"What's the matter, dear one?"

"Sometimes I don't feel good."

"Hmmm, let me take a look at you.
Well, you look fine, sound fine, all your parts
are working. Everything seems to be in order.
Tell me, what kind of thoughts have you
been thinking lately?"

"The usual. Trying not to let the turkeys
get me down, keep my head above water,
you know, stuff everyone thinks. Just wanting
to get by, hold my own, survive."

"Aha, just as I thought. You've been thinking
like everyone else, so now you feel like
everyone else, kind of "blah."

"Well, here's a little trick. Stop trying to make so much sense of things. Stop being so logical. Stop thinking that the future depends upon what has been, or even what appears 'to be.' The props of your life are just props, fictional. You're not at the mercy of the past, the present, or the future . . . logic, reason, or rationales. You are a Being of Light for whom all things remain possible, and there are no caveats to this truth.

"Feel better? Good."

Dr. Universe, Rx #77

Close? You are so close
it's actually painful for those who know.

Poor "things." With bated breath they're writhing in anticipation, rolling in the aisles, imploring you to stay the course. They can see what lies in the unseen, they know of the coincidences and accidents that are about to be unsprung, and they know if you could see them too, you'd be unstoppable.

Whatever you do next, please, think of your fans.

Your attention, please . . .

Your attention, please . . .

This . . . is the Universe.

Today I'll be recording your every thought
and emotion, no matter how "good" or "bad," no
matter how generous or stingy, and no matter how
helpful or hurtful it may be. And everything
I record . . . will be played back for you, as soon
as possible, as some type of physical manifestation
in time and space.

Thank you, that is all.

For as long as you are capable
of anger, there are lessons to learn.

Adventurer Advisory
Global Alert!

Do not trust facts!!!! While they appear to be logical and self-proving, they are perhaps at the root of every evil (if you believe in evil). Here are two safeguards that will help keep you out of trouble:

First, do not ever look to facts for answers.

Second, never plan your life around them.

Facts masquerade as reality, when in fact (yuck, yuck) they're little more than stubborn group opinions. Bad "facts"!

Just ignore 'em, and they'll go away.

Give.

A little birdie

just came my way and mentioned a deep,
soulful desire of yours.

Heavens no, not that one!

She said that you'd be eternally grateful if,
once and for all, you never, ever had to worry
about money again.

Well, I couldn't resist. Wish granted! You never,
ever have to worry about money again.

Anything else? Anything at all?

The Universe

You could never spend
all the abundance that's yours to spend.
Your supply is truly limitless.

Of course, of course, you already know that.
The size of your supply isn't the issue. Finding it is.
You know it's there, you know it's yours, and you
know you deserve it. But how to get your hands
on it? That's the challenge.

Aha, "how." Did you just ask "how"? You did.

Oh dear, never ask how. Never think about how;
let go of the hows. If you wonder about how,
it means your consciousness is not dwelling in spirit,
it means you're trying to manipulate matter, and
it means you're gonna be searching for a long,
long, long, long time.

Steer clear of the hows, dear heart,
and simply dwell on the end result.

Got it?

The real reason you chose
to be here—your purpose and mission in life—
was to simply be who you now are.

Good reason.

You want more, and that's good,
very good. More money, love, energy, laughter.

Okay, here's the deal . . . just remember that these
"things" lie only a thought away . . . not a career
away, not a year away, not a lucky break away,
not a relationship away . . . just a thought away.

Okay?

Now, please think those thoughts.

Do you have any idea,
of why I love you so much?

It's because if you were not exactly as you now are, for everything you've been through, I would not be exactly as I now am. And there are no words that can express just how much more I am because you are just as you now are.

Oh . . . Gives me the chills.

Wonder no more.

Your grateful comrade in adventure,

The Universe

The trick with imagination,
is remembering to use it.

Visualize every day.

Your wishes

are what the Universe wishes for you.
Your thoughts steer the ship of your dreams.
And no matter where you've "been," or how
challenging your circumstances, right here and
now is all that matters.

You are forever. Invincible. A Being of Light on
an adventure of the highest order: to have fun and
be happy in a magical, infinite, loving reality that
conspires tirelessly in your favor; where thoughts
become things, dreams come true, and all things
remain forever possible.

Any questions?

The reason you're "here"
is not to be good, to be better, to be perfect,
to get "stuff" done, to save the world, to save
somebody, to prove something, or to be
anything . . . other than yourself.

That's all you have to work on. That's all you
can do. But by doing it . . . all those other things
will happen anyway.

It's time you learned the truth.

Actually, you should have been told long, long ago.

You see, there was kind of a mix-up.

Things like this are never easy. But, well, to be as direct as possible . . .

You're not human.

Of course, you probably just think I'm being cute, but the truth, is that you are not human. Not even a little. Not one speck.

Now, before you go all ape, realize, there's a bright side to everything, and in this case, it's blinding . . .

You no longer have to behave as one.

Tallyho,

The Universe

Someone once said,
"No pain, no gain."
And so it became their reality.

Bummer, huh?

Amazing, simply amazing!

Do you realize that today you may or may not receive certain phone calls, compliments, e-mails, surprises, letters, or visitors? Do you realize that today you may or may not receive word of good or bad news? Do you realize that today you may or may not encounter certain challenges, triumphs, problems, or victories?

And to think, you're the one who decides.

Wow.

Be good to yourself.

If they're in your life,
love them.

When you understand someone,
truly understand someone, no matter who they are,
you cannot help but love 'em, even though you
might not always love what they do.

You knew that.

Okay. Just as true is that for anyone you feel less
than love for, no matter who they are, it's because
you do not truly understand them.

(No, you don't have to like what they do either,
nor are you "supposed" to stay with them.
You get to decide those things.)

Your supply is the Universe,
and its ways are infinite.

Of all the joys on earth,
few compare to the crowning glory of achieving
against the odds, succeeding in the face of peril,
or triumphing over adversity.

Wouldn't you say?

Yet in every such case, without exception,
the poor odds, the peril, and the adversity
must come first.

Feeling blessed?

Be yourself.

Not who you're supposed to be, but who you want to be. Not their way, but your way. And everything else will take care of itself.

Do not think

that you have to get "there," wherever "there"
is for you, with what you have today, whether in
terms of money, confidence, talent, connections,
whatever. Doesn't work like that. Too scary.

Bad idea.

Once you set yourself in motion, the necessary
resources—in terms of money, confidence, talent,
connections—will be drawn to you.

[Soft whisper in the background,
"Once you set yourself in motion . . ."]

Fade out.

Here's a little workshop
on how to manifest absolutely anything . . .

1. "Ask" once.

2. Give thanks often.

End of workshop.

What if it was true
that you make your own reality, and that your
thoughts became the things and events of your life?

What would you do differently in the next five
minutes? In the next five days?

Time out! Time out!

What do you mean, it doesn't seem like it's working? You can't see your life turning around? It's hard? Ack!

Of course, it doesn't seem like that; of course, it seems hard! This is an adventure, you're an adventurer, and uncertainty and setbacks "happen." Besides, "easy" has never been your style, and setbacks are only ever stepping-stones to grander places.

The day your ship arrives, and it now swiftly approaches, the journey and the setbacks will be among your fondest memories.

Stay the course!

Resume play,

The Universe

PS—Challenges? Problems? Big deal!

It does little good to say
you want something and then, "just in case,"
prepare to do without.

Burn your bridges.

Did you realize

that whenever you gave anything, to anyone,
you gave to the entire world?

And did you realize that for every path
you've walked, for every stone you've turned over,
and for every door you've knocked on, you did so
for everyone?

And finally, did you realize that whenever you felt
love, for any reason whatsoever, you irrevocably
lifted the entire planet higher into the light?

Thanks, from all of us.

Logic is overrated.

Big time.

There's always a way.

Do you know what happens
just before something really incredible takes place?
Something mind-blowing? Just before a really
huge dream comes true?

Do you?

Nothing.

Nothing happens. At least not in the
physical world.

So if, perchance, right now, it appears that
absolutely nothing is happening in your life . . .
consider it a sign.

All roads lead to truth,
though some will take you there a whole heck
of a lot quicker than others.

Be honest with yourself.

This is the Universe,
and as part of this week's celebrations,
I'm going to share a little secret with you.
Actually, I should have shared it with you ages
ago, but most "people" aren't ready for this
kind of secret. I've decided you're different.

It's the secret to getting anything, absolutely
anything you want. Okay? To magnetizing
into your life the things, emotions,
and circumstances you dream of. All right?
It explains how masters become masters and
adepts become adepts. And it'll finally convince
you that I am always there to lend a hand
or perform a miracle. Cool?

Practice.

Yeah, practice. Because just a little practice
goes farther than you could ever imagine.

PS—Now fight the temptation to nod and shrug it off. Do something! Visualize just a little. Act with faith just a little. Explore your beliefs just a little. Manifest a little something; a phone call, a compliment, a flower, whatever. Expect a little miracle. Expect a little help. Expect it to be easy.

Practice.

The Universe knows how.

Adventurers All-Points Bulletin

Have you discovered yet how some angels—like the ones who heal with their smiles, who help light the way for others, and in whose path the flowers gently sway—are actually disguised as people?

And have you also noticed that some of them don't even know they're angels?

Psssssst! This one was written for you.

What if there was only you,
and the rest of the world was "make-believe,"
imagination? If even the people in your life
were drawn there, or faded away, based upon
your thoughts.

Would it then be easier for you to grasp the
true meaning of limitless? Would you then
believe that you alone make your reality?

Dearest, the rest of the world is "make-believe,"
imagination. And all the people in your life are
there or fade away based upon your thoughts.

WOW . . . that was easy.

Tallyho, limitless.

Don't let those
who aren't in tune with you,
distract you from those who are.

How much longer

before you revel in the awareness that you are
enough, that you've done enough, and that you're
now worthy of your heart's greatest desires?

What has to happen for you to give
this to yourself?

No biggie. Just wondering. Take your time.

You chose your dreams

for the journeys they'd inspire, and you knew
when you chose them that there'd be obstacles,
dark days, and knuckleheads who'd stand in
your way. They're part and parcel of where
you're headed, and they don't just go away.

So when you face your next challenge, welcome it.
Rise up, don't back down. See it as a stepping-stone,
not a wall; a valley, not an abyss. And before you
know it, as one is conquered after another, the
journey will be complete, and the joy of manifesting
your dream will pale in comparison to the
satisfaction of your persevering, overcoming,
and breaking through.

Don't you see these are the days, right now,
mid-adventure, that will mean the most to you
once your dreams come true?

Enjoy.

Isn't it curious

how people pick others to be in their lives,
at work, at home, and to play, not because they're
perfect, but to have fun, learn, and grow? But then,
shortly after they arrive, they're often unhappy
because those they picked aren't perfect?

What am I missing?

No one in your shoes
could have done better than you've done,
with where you began, what you had, and all
you've been through. No one.

Aren't you glad it wasn't easier?

Can you imagine the joy,
the peace, the complete sense of satisfaction?
The harmony, the love, and stitches of laughter?
Can you imagine the interest income?!

Good, because nothing else shapes mountains,
people, and bank accounts quite like imagination.

Ka-ching.

It's the thirst for approval,
validation, and justification from sources outside
of yourself that blinds you to the fact that they
need not be earned.

Let's pretend, just for today,
all day long, throughout our every thought and
decision, that life is easy, that everyone means well,
and that time is on our side. Okay?

And let's pretend that we are loved beyond belief,
that magic conspires on our behalf, and that nothing
can ever hurt us without our consent.

All right?

And if we like this game, we'll play tomorrow
as well, and the next day, and the next,
and pretty soon, it won't be a game at all, because
life, for us, will become those things. Just as
it's become what it is, today.

Thoughts become realities, too.

Today, you will be challenged.

Challenged by the grand illusion.
Tempted to look to time, space, and all things
material for understanding; to judge your place in
the world; and to make decisions about your life.

Fight it.

Go within.

Remember the magic.

Be vigilant.

Imagine watching TV

and you see a German shepherd at the beach with a tennis ball in its mouth. Suddenly, with a subtle flick of its head, the dog throws the ball with pinpoint accuracy to its master 100 feet away. Or you watch a program where you see a Ferrari traveling at 160 mph, headed straight for a group of people standing in the middle of the road, eating shrimp and caviar, and at the precise point necessary, the car rapidly decelerates, abruptly stopping less than a single millimeter before disaster, and no one flinches.

What kind of TV do you watch, anyway?

Your brain wants to say "no way," because it wants logic and the physical senses to interpret reality, but the cinematographers have you in the palm of their hands, unbound by rules, free to play films in reverse, without telling you.

The Universe is the same,
its trump card lies in orchestrating an unseen reality
that escapes both logic and the physical senses.

It's as if the Universe works backward, too.
You think of the end result, what you want to
happen in your life, and then the Universe works
backward, aligning your dreamed-of life with where
you are today, stringing together people, places,
and events, for the "impossible" to become possible.

This is how life works.

Trust the Universe, it knows how. Don't tie
its hands with logic, fear, or limiting beliefs.
And next year the Oscar for trick photography . . .
could be yours.

What if all the people
in your life, every single one of them,
even the pesky ones, asked to be there,
so that your light might brighten their way?

It's so tempting

to look at your present life situation, at whom you're with, at where you work, at what you have and have not, and think to yourself, "This was obviously meant to be, I'm here for a reason." And to a degree, you'd be right. But you are where you are because of the thoughts you used to (and may still) think, and so you are where you are to learn that this is how life works—NOT because it was meant to be.

Don't give away your power to vague or mysterious logic. Tomorrow is a blank slate in terms of people, work, and play, though because it, too, will be of your making, you will again have that sense that it was meant to be, no matter who or what you've drawn into your life.

Nothing is meant to be, except for your freedom to choose and your power to create.

Choose big and be happy.

Do you think the Universe
ultimately rewards those who live in poverty? Do
you think those who toil and sweat from paycheck
to paycheck are more likely to inherit the Kingdom
than those who work in ivory towers? Does the
Universe take special notice of sacrifices?
Is it pleased when some put the needs of others
before their own? Does the Universe favor
those who strive to live spiritual lives?

Actually, honey, the Universe doesn't give
a flying yahoo. It loves you no matter
what rules you make up.

Talk about unconditional.

It's your degree of faith,
your belief in benevolent powers and
events unseen, that summons the magic,
either in huge gobs or in drips and drops.

Go for gobs, it costs the same.

Visualizing for Beginners . . .

For those who want convenient
parking spaces, unexpected gifts, or chance
encounters with cool people:

First, think. Second, let go.

Visualizing for the Illuminated . . .

For those who want a healing touch,
world peace, or a new Bentley Azure:

First, think. Second, let go.

Choose carefully.

Dues?

Those were all taken care of eons ago!
You don't have any more dues to pay!

I know, I know, you don't believe it.

Okay, Plan B. You do have dues to pay. You must slave and scrimp, wriggle and pimp, work overtime, pound the pavement, sacrifice, barter, and be selfless. Endure the stupidity of others, work a job you don't love, and unlearn a lifetime of bogus teachings.

Are these the dues you believe in? Well, then, haven't you paid these, too, ten times over?

It's as if you won
the Universe's "Live the Absolute Life
of Your Dreams" lottery, a long, long,
long time ago. But instead of finally checking
your ticket . . . you keep on buying more . . .
hoping, wishing, and praying.

Think of everyone
on the planet, everyone, as your
special friend . . .

And so they shall become.

Dang.

Do you think
that the Universe longs to
"Give you the Kingdom"?

Well, it doesn't.

You see, Your Highness, that transaction
took place absolutely ages ago.

Tallyho.

Just a reminder
in case you forgot, in case you've thought
otherwise, or in case you never knew . . .

There is nothing you can't have.

There is nothing you can't do.

There is nothing you can't be.

Okay?

Whoa! Happy days! Rock on!

I just read about you in the Universal Times!
The Universal Times! Sure enough, there you were,
picture and all, ". . . this exemplary Being of Light,
residing on planet Earth"—I said to myself,
"I know that Being of Light!!"—"has been awarded
the Double-Secret Medal of Honor for bravery
and valor in seeing through the illusions of
Time and Space!"

Now, this is no little thing! It's huge! Because even
while "Time~Space" is a primitive school, it's still
the most hypnotic adventure ever dreamed up.
In fact, only the most courageous are even allowed
to participate. And of these, only a teensy, tiny
percentage ever come to realize that it's all illusions;
that they craft their own destinies; and that in spite
of all physical appearances to the contrary, any life
can turn around on a dime. Fewer still receive
the Double-Secret Award!

My word, you are extraordinary, and it's about time you received the recognition you deserve. But there's a reason it's "double-secret." If you share this news with lesser mortals . . . let's not go there.

Shhhhhh.

Tallyho,

The Universe

PS—You looked smashing in white, but what's with the hat and feathers?

PPS—Now, remember why you won.

What good does it do

knowing approximately where the treasure lies,
yet never digging? Having a bank account
with millions in it, but never writing a check?
Or discovering the fountain of youth,
but never drinking a drop?

You must live the truths you discover, you must
break your old rules, defy logic, be the change.
Dig, write the check, and drink eternally,
one little step after another.

I'm sorry, but there's no other way.

Tallyho,

The Universe

PS—Of course, you can ask for help.

Question: What would it take,
what would have to happen in your life these days,
for you to allow yourself to really kick back,
relax, and just enjoy?

Answer: Whatever it is, whatever, you will
achieve it, earn it, acquire it, or experience
it so much faster if you first kick back,
relax, and just enjoy.

Simple enough?

Good news!

By virtue of your brave presence in Time and Space, an often challenging and sometimes even frightful arena, you're prequalified for platinum Universal assistance.

This coverage is unlike any other on the market. As a Time~Space Adventurer, you have at your disposal our unlimited resources, invisible principles, and trillions of years of experience, momentum, and overhead.

We can solve any problem, intervene in any crisis, and, quite effortlessly, shock and delight the senses at a moment's notice. And best of all, this coverage is free, eternal, and irrevocable. In fact, even if you wanted to, you couldn't leave home without it.

In order to activate your coverage, simply give thanks. Thanks in advance that the help you stand in need of has already been provided.

Please, be our guest, enjoy these privileges that you so richly deserve.

Here's the thing:

It—whatever "it" is for you, relationships,
money, life—will never, ever, be easy . . .
until you first begin thinking of "it" as easy.

Chic-a-boom,

The Universe

You see, it's the same
with everything. It must happen in thought first.
It must. Even when, especially when, by all outer
appearances, your desires seem preposterous.

Anyone can think happy thoughts when they're
happy, wealthy thoughts when they're wealthy,
healthy thoughts when they're healthy.

Your life's mission was to create the stage
you're now on so that you'd have reason to
awaken from your slumber. To have dreams worth
pursuing and the passion to press on in spite of the
conditions surrounding you. To learn you must look
beyond your illusions and grasp that your dreams
are indeed what's meant to be.

This is the Holy Grail. Your search is over.
Go out on a limb, give it your unending best,
and never, ever, ever give up. There haven't been
any accidents, you haven't made any mistakes,
and the perfection is excruciating—you'll see.

Carry on, brave heart.

What if, what if suddenly,
in a flash of fire and light, you got it! And among
other things, you suddenly understood, without
a doubt, the creative power of your word.
Do you think you'd ever again utter, "it's hard,"
"it's not working," "something's wrong with me,"
or "I don't know"?

Nope, you wouldn't, not ever again.

Using your physical senses
to assess your options is kind of like driving
while looking in the rearview mirror. Not too swift,
unless you want to go backward.

Mostly, the physical senses show what has been,
not what will be. For direction, look within.
To your feelings, your heart, and, most important,
your dreams.

Though I must admit, you do look
smashing in mirrors.

Do you know why you are you?

Because no one else could be.

Of course there are "things" you
want that you don't yet have!

They're why you're here.

Today treat everyone
exactly the way you would treat them as if you
had already "arrived," because behind their eyes,
the Universe is watching, looking for direction,
as it paints each moment of time.

Do DO Do Doo Do DO Do Doo . . .

Do you realize that for any
dream of yours to come true, the dreams of others
take huge leaps forward? Not just indirectly,
but directly. People like partners, family members,
your agent, your reps, your suppliers, your custom-
home builder, your publisher, and so many more.
Even people you don't yet know. Then, as their
dreams advance, the dreams of their associates are
advanced, and then their associates, and then theirs,
and so on, and so on.

What's really cool is that way deep down, they all
know this ahead of time and they all know you.
In fact, whenever you dream and move with those
dreams, those among the masses whose own dreams
are aligned with and complement yours are
psychically summoned. Pacts are formed, deals are
made, and coincidences calculated. Odds increase
exponentially, and risks are minimized (if you
believe in odds and risks). And you are propelled
even farther and faster by their energy as well
as your own.

In fact, I was actually asked
to write this Note to you on behalf of all those
whose lives will be dramatically enhanced by your
dreams coming true. Your team, as it were.

Embrace criticism,
whether from the wise or from fools.
Never has a word been uttered that didn't
have meaning to those who heard it.

Anger closes the mind
and cools the heart at a time when both
are needed most.

Hubba, Hubba, Hubba!

Ya know how the bud of a flower looks?
Already attractive, special, and unique
yet still barely hinting at the splendor and
magnificence to come. Oblivious itself of how
its presence will add to the world.

That's what you remind me of.

The Universe

That's right. This is a dream.

You're still asleep. Any minute now, an elephant might appear behind you wearing a pink tutu and tennis shoes. Or maybe the phone will ring, and it'll be Abraham Lincoln to ask why you're late for the ball. Or perhaps Oprah is down the hall, live audience in tow, about to introduce you as her new favorite author. Anything can happen in a dream, anything, without regard to the past, without regard to logic, and you never have to figure out the "hows."

Learn from your dreams, because the stuff of time and space is no different. Forget your past. Pitch the logic. And drop the cursed hows.

Tallyho,

The Universe

PS—Cute whiskers.

Can you imagine having

made a difference in so many lives that people everywhere talk about you for the rest of their lives?

Can you imagine truly leaving the world a better place than you found it? Can you imagine that all the angels might know your name?

You have. It's done. They do.

Good God almighty, what are you gonna do next?

Just one of your many fans,

The Universe

PS—And you're so young!

You—yes, you holding this book—
are the one who was sent to make a difference,
to be a bridge, to light the way, by living the truths
that have been revealed to you, so that others
might do the same.

Now do you know why you've always seen
the world so much more clearly than others?

To help.

This is the Universe,
and have I got some "goodish" news for you
(the "ish" isn't so good)!

The good news—you know the stuff you want:
wealth and abundance, friends and laughter,
I think you once said a fabulous house on the lake?
Well, it's all done . . . hurray!

Your burning desires, the intense yearnings
you've felt, the highly pitched longing, and your
silent pining for these things and more have actually
created this world . . . in another dimension.

(That's part of the "ish.")

In fact, I can see a "probable" you there now,
lolling about in the lap of luxury, giggling and then
roaring with laughter, doing the "lawn mower,"
"high-fiving" your friends, and them all turning
various shades of green with envy. You know,
you're a real hoot when you're so happy.

But there's more "ish." Seems the yearning and pining have actually distanced you from this reality you've created. You see, thoughts of "I want, I want, oh God, how I want" are picked up by the Universe, me, as "I don't have, I don't have, oh God, how I don't have," and then these thoughts manifest, as all thoughts do, perpetuating the lack!

To remove the "ish," here's the dish: Start with the "thank you, thank you, oh God, thank you," and behave accordingly.

Mow on, maestro,

The Universe

And sometimes you wonder
whether or not you've been realistic, whether
or not it's within you, whether or not "it" really
works. But in your wondering, you've given pause
to an entire Universe that never once thought to
doubt and yet still is poised to deliver.

Pop Quiz

Q: How do you find love, health, abundance, or enlightenment?

A: Stop searching. And start seeing what's been there all along.

There are no tough times,
hard knocks, or challenges that aren't laden with
emeralds, rubies, and diamonds for those who see
them through.

Isn't it a hoot?

Of all the people in all the world who actually
"get it," few, if any, actually give it to themselves.

The trick? Baby steps.

Give, just a little, today. Give credit, give praise,
give goodies to yourself, and the Universe
will give you even more.

Selfishness is a virtue, unless you think it must
come at the expense of others. And why would
anyone think that? Oh yeah, that's what all the
people who don't "get it" told you.

You are ready.

The secret to getting rich
is knowing that you already are and acting like it.

PS—Darling, do tell me who manages your assets.
And those gems! Are they real?

(Answer: The Universe, and real what?)

All you have to do

is be. Be yourself.

There's nothing to prove. And there's no one to please who isn't already over the moon with joy at how well you've done and with who you've become.

Uh-oh . . .

Good news and bad news again.

First, the bad news. In the days, weeks, and months ahead you're very likely gonna have the same dang problem that you have today.

Now the good news. The only real problem you have today is thinking that you have problems.

You just don't.

The Universe

Someone so cool,
something so neat, and somewhere so wonderful
are all on the menu. You just have to make up
your mind and order.

And you should see dessert . . .

You must use what you've got.

Talent, brains, heart. Instincts, hunches, feelings.
Money, health, friendships. Time, space, stuff.

Otherwise, why would more be given?

You rock,

The Universe

Limits are for those
who don't believe in the Universe.

Knock, knock. _____ _____?

It's me, the Universe, and I've heard a little rumor.

Seems someone on earth is asking for their own fabulous home in the country!!!! Phew, wouldn't that be nice! Know anyone?

I thought so. Well, guess what?

I have one, and it's ready for delivery!

Would you do me a little favor?

Would you tell them that in order to get it from here to there, all they have to do is close their eyes, count to three, click their heels, give thanks that it's already in their life, and begin moving toward it?

No, no. Some of that's "make believe," but so is their fabulous home in the country until they stop asking and start giving thanks and moving toward it.

Tallyho,

The Universe

PS—Do something.

Can you feel
your heart beating?

It's beating in threes today.

Go on, right now, feel it.

It's saying, "I~^ love~^ you~^!"

And it really does.

Understanding . . .

is the elixir of life.

If you could see just how life
was meant to be . . . you'd probably faint.

Because things would look exactly like they look today, and you'd find that you are exactly where you're "supposed" to be, in an adventure without end.

It's okay to love material things;
matter is pure spirit, only more so.

And on Friday, the Universe said,
"Yo! Ho! Ho! It's time to have fun!"

Whereupon it invented imagination, and there was
a huge gasp among the angels. For it was clear that
the reins of power in Time and Space had been
passed to those so blessed, and that they would
be left to discover this for themselves.

And it was good.

Happy anniversary!

PS—And as the angels quickly gathered,
there, in line, stood you.

Your attention, please . . .

Your attention, please . . .

This . . . is the Universe.

Would whoever gave thanks for a home on the lake, more friends, and a couple of million bucks please specify which lake, what kind of friends, and provide some kind of general time frame?

Hul-lo?

Details. If they don't know, how can I?

You've been worthy.

You are worthy. You'll be worthy.

Of course,
"Here & Now" is what really matters, but people
will be people, so . . . given that you're a FOREVER
BEING, I do hope you're spending as much time
looking forward as you are looking back.
Because really, forever means you have quite
a lot to look forward to.

Here's a snippet of advice
that comes from an as yet undiscovered manuscript
buried deep in some Pyrenees mountain cave . . .

"Choose feelings over logic, adventure over
perfection, here over there, now over then,
and always love, love, love."

It also said "you rock," but you never
would have believed that.

If time and space are illusions . . .
doesn't that mean you come "from" and now
exist in a "place" that "precedes" both?

Wouldn't this then mean that you're
really everywhere, always?

It does, and you are . . .
UNLIMITED beyond your wildest imaginings.

If the Universe suddenly appeared before you in the form of a wise, old, kindly messiah with a glowing white aura and presented you with a one-hundred-point game plan that would guarantee, guarantee your dreams coming true but first required that you let go of all your worldly possessions, shave your head, walk on a bed of nails, sacrifice three hours every day training your mind, and invest a minimum of two years before you began to see the first changes, would you follow the plan? Would you follow it if all of your dreams would then come true?

Did you say yes? I know you said yes.

Now, if the Universe suddenly appeared before you on the pages of this book, spoke to your heart, and said that in order to begin living the life of your dreams within one year or less, all you had to do was imagine the life of your dreams (visualize five minutes a day), move with the life of your dreams (with a token act of faith performed just once a day), and honestly face your fears, would you even try?

Hmmmm.

If visualizing were extremely difficult, maybe then people would do it. Oh yeah, they'd form clubs, give designations, have car washes!

You wouldn't believe
the stuff people think they want.

Just the other day someone was asking for a llama.

Nothing wrong with llamas, I have a few myself,
but the llama he wants is supposed to help him with
his business; schlepping stuff over mountains,
they're good for that.

Now, why do you suppose he
didn't just ask for a pickup truck?

Trust me, he could've asked for a pickup truck,
and he'd have been a lot happier.

So . . . I'm off to the bazaar. In the meantime,
should you need anything, please be sure to ask
for what you really want.

The good thing
about bad things is that they make way
for even better things.

When you stop and reflect
that thoughts become things, unconditionally,
without exception, no matter what, no matter
whose, and you grasp that this is an immutable law
that throws the entire Universe into overdrive on
your behalf, don't you just want to cry for those who
still keep looking for answers?

Me, too.

When you look at old photos

it's obvious, isn't it? You were good-looking back then. Really good-looking. Yet somehow, at the time, you didn't quite believe it.

Learn from yesterday, because today you're even better looking than you were then. Way better. You're smarter, too. Funnier. Wiser. More compassionate, less serious. And you're finally sauntering!

Just thought you should know.

If you only knew

just how literally true all of these Notes are—
concerning your power, your strength, and your
divinity, about the love, the magic, and the infinite
possibilities—for the next few days you'd see the
rest of the world . . . through tears.

And you'd never stop giving thanks.

Ain't life grand?